## UNDER STRESS

Grueling training in tropic heat . . . long labor in sub-freezing polar regions constant . . . high-level noise . . . sickness-inducing motion—these are among the severest stresses we can encounter. Controlled studies have shown that Siberian ginseng can protect against the effects of these and other stresses, as well as acting as a tonic and immune system stimulant. Here is the latest scientific information on this multipotent herb and how it can be of use to you.

## ABOUT THE AUTHOR

**Betty Kamen, Ph.D.** is coauthor, with Lynn Fraley, R.N., Dr. P.H., of *Nutrition in Nursing: The New Approach*, the Good Health Guide *Sesame*, with her husband, Si Kamen, of *Total Nutrition During Pregnancy, Kids Are What They Eat*, and many other works on health and nutrition. She and Si Kamen have produced nationally recognized health-related TV shows and filmstrips.

# Siberian Ginseng

## Latest research on the fabled Oriental tonic herb

Betty Kamen, Ph.D.

Keats Publishing, Inc.  New Canaan, Connecticut

*Siberian Ginseng* is not intended as medical advice. Its intention is solely informational and educational. Please consult a medical or health professional should the need for one be indicated.

SIBERIAN GINSENG

ISBN: 0-87983-485-4

Printed in the United States of America

Good Health Guides are published by
Keats Publishing, Inc.
27 Pine Street (Box 876)
New Canaan, Connecticut 06840

# CONTENTS

# INTRODUCTION

"Now I see the secret of the making of the best persons. It is to grow in the open air, and to eat and sleep with the earth." This pronouncement by Walt Whitman in *Leaves of Grass* suggests a world far removed from our fast-paced, highly technological society. Although most of us cannot live an earth-life to become the best that we can be, we can benefit from substances that thrive in just that kind of milieu. The root of a wild shrub that grows abundantly in the Far East offers that potential.

Imagine for a moment that you are living in pre-drugstore days. No phones, no hospitals. Worse—no commercials on TV, radio, or in print to inform you of the latest headache antidote or lack-of-energy remedy. So it was for time immemorial. Good health practices, accumulated from struggles with illness and wise observation, were handed down from generation to generation in folk application. No sophisticated analytical methods revealed the scientific basis of the accepted health system. Empirical evidence was the guideline.

The concept of "wholeness" formed the foundation for the special systems of therapy that held fast over the years, particularly in Asian medicine: disease, although it appears to be specific in presentation, is caused by a general reduction in resistance. Based on this reasoning, Asian medicine emphasized the importance of taking an all - purpose "tonic," to maintain vigor and vitality and to recover strength to overcome sickness.

Ginseng has long been esteemed as the ultimate tonic strengthens and supports body health. It has even been reputed to build ambition. An ancient Chinese herbalist is quoted as saying, "Person would rather take handful of ginseng than cartload of gold and jewels."[1]

# THE PRIZE VARIETY

The family of plants to which ginseng belongs is not less than 150 million years old. At least four thousand years ago, the first Chinese treatise on medicine refers to it. In 200 A.D., the Emperor Cho-Chi-Kiu described ginseng as a panacea. No wonder ginseng has been called the "root of life."

Ginseng is no longer a mystical herb of the Orient. In fact, it is a major export of the United States. In 1981, "Growing Ginseng" was one of the most popular farmer bulletins dispensed by the Department of Agriculture.

Not all ginseng is alike, however; many varieties abound. If you want the most efficacious ginseng, *Eleutheroccocus senticosus* is the choice. *Eleutherococcus senticosus* was selected for economic development and for distribution as a supplement after extensive studies of ginseng varieties. It is the prize of all ginseng breeds, and should not be confused with Chinese, Korean, or other types. Although Eleutherococcus and other ginseng have very similar pharmacological properties, Eleutherococcus exerts the greater prophylactic and healing effects.[2]

Formerly known as *Hedera senticosa* and *Acanthopanax senticosus*, *Eleutherococcus senticosus* is commonly called Siberian ginseng, and is also referred to as "touch-me-not," "devil's shrub," "spiny eleutherococc," "wild pepper" or just plain "eleuthero." Some of the names describe its character: the plant is spiked with thorns.

*Eleutherococcus senticosus* and ginseng are actually two different plants belonging to the same botanical family. The eleutherococcus senticosus has come to be known as Siberian ginseng through common usage of the term. This book is about *Eleutherococcus senticosus*, but for clarity, simplicity, and familiarity, it will be referred to as Siberian ginseng.

Today, Siberian ginseng root is well known as a medicine claimed to prolong life in the traditional therapies of Southeast Asian countries, where many people begin to take it while in their forties. Successful use by Russian athletes and cosmonauts created an awareness of its energy-giving attributes all over the world in the 1960s. Millions in the Soviet Union alone use Siberian ginseng regularly. The number of consumers increases as the result of each new study showing favorable results—and there have been thousands—is released.[3]

## THE CLASSIC ADAPTOGEN

Substances which help to normalize body functions indirectly and to withstand the diverse stresses of our time are known as adaptogens. An adaptogen promotes rapid mobilization of your body's energy and swift recovery following stress. It is not only therapeutic, but also preventive, a broad-action tonic. Ginseng has the well-deserved reputation of being the classic adaptogen—honored with this title after 189 plants had been studied.[4]

Adaptogens
* are non-toxic
* have no marked pharmacologic effects
* are nonspecific in their results
* enhance ability to cope with:
  physical stress
  emotional stress
  biochemical stress
* do not require prescriptions
* are user-friendly (no professional expertise required for administration)
* are less costly than most drugs
* are not habit forming
* regulate; they are held in abeyance when challenge ceases to exist, but are ready and waiting for the next crisis

Adaptogens consider biochemical individuality. They affect different people in distinct ways as they interact with diet, lifestyle, exercise, exposure to environmental toxins and drug intake (both recreational and medicinal). Adaptogens are used primarily to increase resistance, health and vitality.

## GROWING THE BEST OF THE BEST

Regardless of efforts to "garden" ginseng and grow it under controlled conditions, the undomesticated wild plant remains the thoroughbred, a product of the inscrutable wisdom of nature—having a higher range and force of action. Like most everything else, the more natural, the more superior.

The best Siberian ginseng grows in organically rich soil in an environment free of chemicals, pollutants and pesticides. Natural resources of Siberian ginseng can be found in eastern Russia and northern Japan. How lucky we are to be able to purchase wild Siberian ginseng, imported from the Far East—meticulously prepared to preserve every crucial nutrient and property of this remarkable plant.

I visited Hokkaido, the northernmost island of Japan, and stood on the mountainside surrounded by an explosion of wild Siberian ginseng plants. I saw the shrubs with tall, erect stems and densely covered branches—old gray ones and brownish young ones—thick with fine prickles. And saw beautiful, ripened clusters of black berries. I learned about the problems of self-propagation (up to 80 percent of the seeds are underdeveloped). Temperature is of course important, but aeration and humidity are critical. For normal development of seedlings, shading is necessary, and that's why only certain areas are conducive to the successful growth of this manna from the mountainside.

Steep, wooded valleys run north and south. The rising sun in the east illuminates the western side of the mountain, while the eastern slope is shaded. In the afternoon, the process is reversed; the east is bathed in sunlight and the west shaded. This precise ratio of sun to shade is what works best for Siberian ginseng. It is never found on dry southern slopes and rarely in dense, shadowy forests.

I saw how the product is harvested with special care, at the peak of excellence after years of growth—efforts to maintain its natural integrity. To prevent decomposition of the plant's glycosides (vital constituents explained below), the root must be dried rapidly and stored under specific conditions. I investigated immaculate factories in which ginseng is selected, powdered, and tableted. Roots with the slightest aberration or sign of disease are discarded. It was not unlike watching a platoon of Marines in full dress, standing inspection just before an important parade.

## VALIDATION

Claims made for Siberian ginseng are supported by current research from all parts of the globe. Functions proved by scientific studies are consistent with historical postulates of Chinese herbalists. Chemical properties, biochemical activity, pharmacological actions and clinical effects have been examined. According to published data, Siberian ginseng can reduce the incidence of illness from influenza and acute respiratory diseases to hypertension and angina.

Siberian ginseng has been shown to protect against radiation, to reduce the concentration of sugar in the urine of diabetic animals and to heal wounds. When taken along with other nutrient supplements, it has the unique ability to enhance their assimilation.

Investigation demonstrates that ginseng improves ability to solve problems, concentration, accuracy and speed. The more tired and confused, the stronger the effect.

Here are specific studies which reveal how ginseng is able to pull humanity up from infirmity and to improve wellbeing.

(1) Siberian ginseng and toxins. In 1981, Siberian ginseng was shown to reduce the narcotic effects of long-acting sedatives (such as barbiturates and ether). Ginseng shortens the duration of sleep induced in test animals by these traditional drugs.[5]

Irradiated mice treated with Siberian ginseng survived five times longer than controls.

Other data describe useful applications in acute and chronic poisoning with some insecticides and industrial toxins. Although Siberian ginseng cannot reduce toxicity of all foreign chemical compounds, a majority of substances undergo metabolic inactivation in its presence. It appears to stimulate special enzymes which promote elimination of toxic foreign substances from your body, inactivating xenobiotics. (*Xeno* means foreign or strange; *biotics* denotes living organisms. Xenobiotics are drugs, food additives, alcohol, residual pesticides, and so on; these substances appear to be toxic for sexual cells and human embryos.) The mechanism involved is closely linked with the immune system. It includes a complex of specialized enzymes which help your body to maintain chemical homeostasis.

The following chart shows the effect of a single administration of Siberian ginseng on resistance to a microbial toxin.[6]

| Preparation | Percentage of animals surviving | | | |
| | 24 hrs | 48 hrs | 72 hrs | 96 hrs |
| | after administering microbial toxin | | | |
| --- | --- | --- | --- | --- |
| **Control Solution** | **100** | **0** | **0** | **0** |
| **Siberian Ginseng Extract** | **100** | **70** | **30** | **20** |

All the animals in this study were given a lethal dose of a toxic substance. The animals fortified with Siberian ginseng survived much longer than the controls.

**(2) Siberian ginseng and sexual function.** Siberian ginseng has gonad-stimulating activity. Studies with test animals report increases in weight of the prostate gland and seminal vesicles by 118 and 70 percent respectively. It also promotes estrogenic activity in immature female mice.

Studies conducted with cows and bulls demonstrate improved reproductive capacity of the bulls, with a 28 percent increase of semen production.

The number of eggs laid by hens fed Siberian ginseng for a month increased by 133 percent.[7,8]

The powdered ground root increased the fertility of mating minks.

It is theorized that adaptogens increase total body immunity, making sexual cells more resistant to toxic factors in the environment. A Chinese medical text, dating back to 300 A.D., cites ginseng for the preparation of "love potions."

**(3) Siberian ginseng and cancer.** Mice treated with methotrexate (a drug administered to cancer patients), plus Siberian ginseng, were alive two months after administration. Mice treated with methotrexate alone died within 3 to 4 days following drug application.[9]

The ability of Siberian ginseng to potentiate antitumor immunity has been demonstrated experimentally. Administered orally to rodents, Siberian ginseng delays or prevents metastasis (development of secondary tumors), and prevents or delays mammary tumor or leukemia formation both chemically induced and spontaneous.[10]

Patients with cancer of the lip or mouth cavity benefited from Siberian ginseng treatment. A two-year study, during which patients received Siberian ginseng one hour before radiation treatment, showed no side effects, no relapses of disease, and no metastases.[11]

Siberian ginseng is recommended as an adjunct therapy in the complex treatment of cancer of the mammary gland in major hospitals in Japan. Patients treated in the late stages of cancer show improvement in general condition and blood quality.[12,13]

The Petrov Oncological Institute in Leningrad reported success in improving the general health of patients with cancer, reducing the chances of metastasis, and decreasing the debilitating effects of radiation and chemotherapy.

**(4) Siberian ginseng and antibodies.** Administration of Siberian ginseng increased the amount of antibodies in test animals. The ginseng was given every morning for 30 days, and the amount of antibodies remained at a high level for 50 days, demonstrating the ability of Siberian ginseng to increase the immune response. Researchers suggest this study may be very meaningful for providing a method for increasing resistance against infection.[14]

**(5) Siberian ginseng, healthy people, and stress.** According to extensive Soviet research, almost everyone can benefit from the use of this extraordinary, biologically active substance. Healthy people working under difficult conditions may alleviate personal stress.

Stress is experienced by those who work in polluted atmospheres, are immobilized at control desks with machines or instruments demanding emotional and/or physical exertion (like me at this very moment as I sit before my word processor for long hours), alter their latitude and longitude with constant travel, work with deadlines (me again), or work mundane nine-to-five jobs. Noise, vibration, and electromagnetic waves are constantly increasing. Stress impinges on millions of people. Chemical changes that take place in your body to defend you against stress can cause disease and even death. At best, stress is usually a useless expenditure of energy; at worst, it is dangerous.

The Soviet researchers severely stressed animals, illustrating that those treated with Siberian ginseng prior to stress exposure do not show the usual signs of stress. Stress hormones secreted from adrenal glands were measured and compared with animals not treated with Siberian ginseng. Less hormone is released in treated animals. Yet the adrenal glands in these animals have greater hormone-manufacturing capacity. Researchers concluded that when stress occurs, ginseng encourages a faster response for stress hormone release and a more rapid return to normal.[15,16] These studies were repeated at the University of California at Los Angeles, with the same results.

Other studies indicate a pronounced increase in survival rate for animals subjected to a variety of physical and biological stresses. A primary action on stress resistance is repeatedly demonstrated.

Patients—either hospitalized or convalescing at home—experience acute or chronic stress more frequently than the more robust sector of our population. Siberian ginseng is especially beneficial to almost anyone with a health problem, including pre- and postoperative patients.

Siberian ginseng can be a prophylactic for fatigue. It increases work capacity and/or helps to create *joie de vivre*. A favorite of Soviet deep sea divers, mine and mountain rescuers, climbers, explorers, and soldiers, it is also used by factory workers exposed to difficult conditions. More than 2,100 healthy people received Siberian ginseng under various conditions in an effort to determine ability to withstand mild or severe adverse conditions. Here are a few of the reports.

*a. Conditions: High-temperature environment* plus four hours of a light daily work load for nine days. Temperature was 37.7 to 38.5 C (or about 100 degrees F). Result with Siberian ginseng: increased oxygen utilization.[17]

b. *Conditions: Healthy radio-telegraphers subjected to controlled high noise conditions.* Result with Siberian ginseng: Number and speed of radiogram receptions increased. Work improved progressively from day to day. The most significant advantage was recorded from the third day on. The benefit paralleled the improvement of the functional condition of the hearing organs.[18]

c. *Conditions: Skiers with different amounts of training.* Result with Siberian ginseng: increased resistance to hypoxemia (deficient blood oxygen); better tolerance to heavy physical burdens when not appropriately prepared beforehand.

d. *Conditions: Workers in jobs involving physical labor in a publishing house.* Result with Siberian ginseng: improvement in activity of cardiovascular system, ability to work, appetite and general wellbeing in those without marked hypertension.

e. *Conditions: Healthy proofreaders in publishing office.* Result with Siberian ginseng: improvement in quality of proofreading. Time of sensorimotor reactions shortened, and number of errors reduced. Optimal brain function promoted.

f. *Conditions: Physical training for sailors subjected to long periods of elevated temperature* on long sea voyages in the tropics. High temperature and moisture restricted working capacity. Result with Siberian ginseng: increased work capability and normalization of body functions. Reduction of unfavorable functional shifts in central nervous, cardiovascular, and heat regulatory systems.[19,20]

g. *Conditions: Healthy males subjected to conditions designed to induce motion sickness.* Result with Siberian ginseng: Beneficial effect.

h. *Conditions: Factory workers in the Polar Region* where average temperature is -5 degrees C (22 degrees F). Result with Siberian ginseng: Reduction of 40 percent in lost days and 50 percent in general sickness over period of one year.[21]

i. *Conditions: Ship repair workers using vibration tools.* Result with Siberian ginseng: improvement in hearing acuity. Mechanism of action may be improvement of the regulation of energy processes in cerebral cortical hearing centers.

**(6) Siberian ginseng and various disease states.** Studies cited in section 5 established benefits to healthy people. Other analyses have been done using more than 2,200 people who have been diagnosed with at least one illness.

a. *Conditions: Atherosclerosis.* Result with Siberian ginseng: improvement in general feelings; disappearance of pains in heart and chest; reduced blood pressure; reduction in serum cholesterol levels. (Treatment was less effective in patients with high blood pressure.)

Siberian ginseng exerted beneficial effect on certain aspects of protein and fat metabolism. Researchers suggested combined therapy for patients with atherosclerosis.[22]

b. *Conditions: Diabetes mellitus.* Result with Siberian ginseng: Successful treatment. Found to protect the islet apparatus of the pancreas. [22,23]

c. *Conditions: Hypertension (high blood pressure) and hypotension (low blood pressure).* Result with Siberian ginseng: Normalization of arterial blood pressure in both hyper- and hypotensive people.[24]

d. *Conditions: Neurosis with complaints of decreased working abilities, exhaustion, irritability, insomnia, and general unrest.* Result with Siberian ginseng: increase in sense of well-being; production of sound sleep. Normalization of reflexes, pulse, blood pressure and appetite were also experienced. [25]

e. *Conditions: institutionalized patients with neuroses.* Result with Siberian ginseng: Significant benefit.

f. Conditions: Patients experiencing either chronic or acute stress because of illness. Result with Siberian ginseng: Success for preoperative preparation of surgical patients, including those with cancer. Speeds recovery. [26]

**(7) Siberian ginseng and menopause.** Nutrition-oriented healthcare professionals encourage postmenopausal women to try Siberian ginseng supplementation before resorting to hormone-replacement therapy. Ginseng demonstrates estrogenic activity.

Endless additional studies have been conducted. In its versatility, Siberian ginseng normalizes weight change in the thyroid gland for extreme conditions of over-or underactivity. It regulates weight of adrenals and suppresses cholesterol in the liver of test animals fed excessive amounts of cholesterol. Certain kinds of acne are cured. It favors optimal conditions for impulses of the cerebral cortex, helping the thinking, process, and improving both short-and long-term memory. Phenylalanine, an amino acid and an important stress regulator, is assisted in its voyage across the blood-brain barrier.

Hemoglobin levels return to normal in less than half the time following blood donation. Many other processes of self-regulation are maximized.

Because thousands of ginseng studies have been done in recent years, science now understands its adaptogenic features–why it helps to improve the ability of healthy people to deal with stressful situations, how it increases resistance, what factors are involved in its ability to maintain an anti-fatigue effect, and why it makes many sick people better.

## HOW SIBERIAN GINSENG WORKS

All these studies are impressive. They demonstrate that Siberian ginseng accelerates restorative processes after intensive activity and increases resistance to unfavorable external influences. Because it enhances endurance, the athlete is able to extend training without harm. Although not everyone is an athlete, everyone can gain from reaching a higher level of effectiveness of motor activity. Siberian ginseng increases stamina and performance, yet it does not have the side effects of any known stimulant. The stimulative effect begins as soon as half an hour to an hour after ingestion.[27]

The Chinese never regarded ginseng as "curative," but rather as "adjustive"—it is able to keep your body in line despite environmental influences. A drug stimulant affects behavior in most situations, but Siberian ginseng acts predominantly when you are faced with a challenge. How does it work?

Despite our ability to set foot on the moon or have our grammar corrected by computer chips, we do not fully understand many aspects of ginseng's properties. But we have gained some knowledge in recent years, and here are a few of the facts.

At least part of the mechanism for the adaptogenic effect of Siberian ginseng can be attributed to its antioxidant influence, which in turn inactivates free radicals. Free radicals are highly reactive molecules. Although they are important for normal biological processes, they become destructive when they are out of control. Free radicals are considered by most authorities to be the mainspring of endless disease processes, and the major cause of aging. They can be detrimental by bonding with life-giving protein tissue, so that the tissue no longer performs its rejuvenating tasks. Free radicals attack cell membranes, accumulate in fat cells and damage nucleic acids (RNA and DNA). It has been suggested that the main action of Siberian ginseng is its ability to inhibit free radicals.

Researchers believe that Siberian ginseng works by regulating energy, nucleic acid and protein metabolism in your tissues. Under stress, a complex substance is generated in your blood. This complex inhibits energy-giving substances from entering cell membranes and also interferes with normal cell activity. Siberian ginseng contains substances that disrupt this negative process, decreasing the competition and minimizing the deleterious effects of the "bad guys"—the stress-released complex. Now your cells can function normally, despite the stress.[28]

Siberian ginseng allows muscles to release less glycogen, and also preserves other substances which diminish energy. At the same time, mobilization of lipids is accelerated.[29] If all this is confusing, suffice it to say that the data suggest that the regulation of energy underlies the biological action of Siberian ginseng. Since any functional activity requires high expenditure of energy, it is the ability of Siberian ginseng to oversee, guard and control these important energy processes that is the scientific basis of its wide biological range of action.

Here's an example. If you jog for 15 minutes, the activity provokes an inhibition of RNA activity by 50 percent because of competition for energy between the RNA reactions and muscle activity. Siberian ginseng doubles the process of recovery, thereby normalizing the biosynthesis of nucleic acids more rapidly. In other words, Siberian ginseng helps to normalize cell activity.[30]

The exceptional quality of Siberian ginseng to normalize deviations from the norm is attributed to its active principles, glycosides. Glycosides act as drugs, increasing the general nonspecific resistance to diverse chemical, physical, and biological factors, as indicated in the studies cited.[31,32]

## SUMMARY OF BENEFITS OF SIBERIAN GINSENG

- Increases physical endurance under stress
- Prevents reduction of endurance after exposure to heartstressing activity
- Protects against reduced cellular oxygen
- Protects against excessive heat conditions
- Protects against excessive cold conditions
- Protects against radiation exposure
- Protects against viral infection
- Protects against microbial infection
- Augments sexual function
- Helps prevent tumor metastasis
- Favors normalization of neurotransmitter metabolism
- Promotes normal endocrine function
- Functions as a detoxifier, reducing the effect of toxic chemical compounds
- improves visual acuity, color perception and hearing acuity
- increases output per person-hour in work settings requiring attention and nervous tension

# REPORTS OF TOXICITY AND OTHER HAZARDS

Interpreting research can be tricky. Don't be misled by conclusions of studies that appear to contradict empirical observation. Nor should you lose sight of the whole of the picture, or even oppose "gut" reactions. (Gut reactions are based on your personal experience.) That is not to say that scientific study should be discounted, but rather that it should be carefully examined.

As an example, you may read that Siberian ginseng, when taken with vitamins, causes vitamin excretion. One study showed that when people were given Siberian ginseng and several vitamins in combination, this caused an increase in the excretion of vitamins B1 and B2. The Siberian ginseng actually caused a saturation of these vitamins because of its synergistic effect. It increases the body's ability to utilize nutrients, so less is needed, and this is believed to be the cause of the increased excretion. It is unlikely that your body would throw off these nutrients if there were no oversupply. People who take Siberian ginseng on a regular basis exhibit an amazing absence of vitamin- deficiency syndrome. Vitamins B1 and B2 are water-soluble, need to be replaced daily, and are thrown off by your body when in excess, rather than stored.[33]

Another report indicates that ginseng glycosides in concentrated forms are potentially poisonous. Most of the everyday foods you consume contain naturally occurring toxicants—substances which are poisonous when isolated. The list includes toxins found in peas, peanuts, cabbage, mustard seed, bananas, tomatoes, apples, plums, rye and fish. These toxins are generally harmless when part of the natural architecture of the whole food.[34] Siberian ginseng is a safe, nontoxic substance, whether with single or recurring administration. There is no significant effect on hemoglobin or red blood cell count when compared with controls. Nor are there any significant changes in weight, ascorbic acid or cholesterol levels. No adverse effects on animal growth have been shown, nor on pregnancy and lactation. Spotted deer feed on this plant in the spring. Other species of plants in the same family are eaten less readily by animals.[35]

Regular aspirin, which many assume to be completely safe, is substantially more toxic than ginseng.

Close scrutiny of one study with a negative outcome reveals that test animals used in the research developed adverse symptoms because of the high alcohol content in preparations used. The injurious reaction was to the alcohol, not to the ginseng.

Others have reported unfavorable effects only when excessive amounts of ginseng were consumed. Just as one can overdose on water, too much ginseng may not be beneficial, even though it has been shown again and again to have minimal toxicity, if any. No side effects were reported in any of the studies involving more than 2,100 healthy people cited above. The wild variety of Siberian ginseng is reported to be even less toxic than cultivated strains, even under adverse conditions (use of alcohol as base for extraction or overdosing).

As an ancient Chinese pharmacopoeia advised on the taking of Siberian ginseng: "Pay attention to use, and never play mischief with the ginseng." When Siberian ginseng fails to provide the desired and predicted results, it may be that it was picked before the thirty years necessary for top quality, or that it was picked at the wrong time of year. Siberian ginseng is at its best in the fall.

Although reduction of blood pressure is gradual and moderate with the use of Siberian ginseng, it is not effective for those suffering from severe forms of high blood pressure. Ginseng is not recommended for persons whose blood pressure is 180/90 or higher.

When you are faced with a stressful situation, Siberian ginseng suppresses the usual defense reaction of your adrenals. Because the stress reaction is protective, the question is raised as to whether the Siberian ginseng is reducing your ability to cope with stress. This is not the case at all. Siberian ginseng does not block the stress reaction, but improves your energy metabolism to such a degree that you don't require the usual high arousal of the stress mechanism. So it actually decreases the stress reaction itself—and the reaction is automatic.

The capacity of Siberian ginseng to regulate physiological functions automatically—depending on requirements—is a singular property of an adaptogen. This ability explains a wide range of the nonspecific action of Siberian ginseng, plus the normalizing pattern, and also demonstrates its safety.

# SIBERIAN GINSENG AS A SUPPLEMENT

Russians place ginseng in vodka to counteract the effects of the alcohol. Although this may appeal to some of you, there are better suggestions for using Siberian ginseng as a supplement.

Healthy people know that there cannot and must not be a sharp division between food and medicine. When you eat good food, you never obtain just one vitamin or mineral or amino acid, but a wide range of nutrients. An apple, for example, contains the full complement of amino acids (not necessarily in usable ratios, but they are present). Siberian ginseng has a wide assortment of beneficial nutrients. A large number of chemical compounds have been isolated or identified in its root. These compounds include sterols, coumarin, and lignins. They contain glycosides, already described, which are thought to produce the basic biological activity of ginseng. Neither the individual components nor the complete set in extracted form have the full efficiency of the entire natural complex. The action of the whole of Siberian ginseng root is not a simple sum total.

Other constituents in Siberian ginseng are measurable amounts of ascorbic acid (vitamin C), beta carotene, vitamins E, B1, B2 and B12, niacin and essential oils. Analysis of the content of trace elements shows that Siberian ginseng incorporates the most essential calcium, phosphorus, potassium, magnesium, sodium, aluminum, barium, iron, strontium, boron, copper, zinc, manganese, chromium and cobalt. The nutrients appear to favor more rapid normalization of metabolism of such biologically active substances as serotonin (important in mental activity) and acetylcholine (which plays a role in the transmission of impulses from one nerve fiber to another).[36]

Wild Siberian ginseng contains 300 parts per million of germanium, a significant percentage. The role of germanium the living cell has been studied extensively in recent years. The content of germanium may help to explain Siberian ginseng's oxygen-sparing activity and the stimulating effect on the immune system. Germanium enhances interferon production, T-cell synthesis, and macrophage function. Its role as a semiconductor creates electrical energy within the cells.[37]

In recent decades we have isolated and recognized the importance of the single nutrient. Although vitamin A or D or B3 or the mineral calcium—and all other vitamins and minerals—have their place in therapy, there are calculated risks. Fat- soluble vitamins can accumulate; a single B vitamin in megadoses can cause an imbalance of the remainder of the B complex; minerals are interdependent, so an overdose of one may increase or decrease the need for another. None of these disadvantages can be assigned to Siberian ginseng.

About ten years ago, it was shown that the introduction of Siberian ginseng to viral-infected animals proved to be futile. If, however, Siberian ginseng was in the system prior to contact with the virus, cells became resistant to the virus. And although it may not always affect the growth of old metastases, it usually prevents the formation of new ones. The point is that Siberian ginseng should be in the category of health insurance—taken in advance of potential problems. This is analogous to the pay-only-if-well paradigm; the rulers of the ancient Orient paid their physicians only when they, the rulers, were healthy. Apparently the healers of the time not only treated disease, but could sustain health (with Siberian ginseng?).

Wild Siberian ginseng is available in uncoated tablet form (for easier assimilation), packed in vacuum-sealed foil pouches to guarantee freshness. One company packages pure wild Siberian ginseng with licorice root. The licorice blend prevents a bitter aftertaste.

Concentrated tablets are easier to take and are more potent than diluted, beverage-form Siberian ginseng. Liquid extracts usually contain alcohol. Be aware that domestic varieties may not be of optimal benefit because of the precise and lengthy growing requirements.

According to the Journal of the American Medical Association, doses as low as half a gram are reported to be therapeutically effective, and 2 to 3 grams are recommended to achieve behavioral stimulation.[38] (I personally take 2 grams daily.) Larger quantities should be taken under a physician's direction. Children can take 100 milligrams at age one, with increasing increments of 100 milligrams for each year. At age ten, the dosage reaches one gram. Again, check with your pediatrician.

Taken in a single dose, Siberian ginseng produces a stimulant effect, but functions as a tonic when consumed repeatedly over a period of time. Fortunately, we do not live in the Sung dynasty of a thousand years ago, when the value of ginseng was determined by its weight in silver. Siberian ginseng in late twentieth century is moderately priced—far less costly than most drugs.

## SIBERIAN GINSENG AND THE FUTURE

With the growing use of xenobiotics, the protective action of Siberian ginseng may be lifesaving for many. Toxic substances of industry and agriculture and of environmental pollution are increasing. Aspirin, caffeine, nicotine, tranquilizers, antihistamine drugs, antibiotics, and many other substances place us at teratogenic risk. (A teratogen is a substance that causes fetus malformation.)

In recent years, toxins—including carcinogens—were discovered among food additives. Extracts from irradiated potato tubers produce a mutagenic effect on sexual cells of test animals. Volatile components of latex and other compounds produce an inhibitory action on spermatozoa.[39]

Human sexual cells and embryos until recently have been protected from light. Storage of human spermatozoa in cryogenic banks, artificial insemination, and embryo cultivation in test tubes may subject reproductive cells and tissues to light exposure as a side effect.[40]

These hazards are potentially embryotoxic (causing harm to a fetus). An essential feature of Siberian ginseng is its ability to protect against damaging factors in the environment and in the human body. On the facing page is a list of a few embryotoxic substances and the results of studies showing protection benefits of Siberian ginseng [41-45]

Researchers conclude that Siberian ginseng promotes the reduction of the embryotoxic effect of some teratogens. Two researchers used Siberian ginseng successfully to reduce the incidence of acute

| Embryotoxic Substance | Effect of Siberian Ginseng |
|---|---|
| Ionizing radiation | Protection of mice from X- ray radiation |
| Hypoxia (oxygen starvation; may be environmental or systemic) | Protection of mice |
| Toxins | Protection in mice injected with tetanus toxoid |
| Alcohol | Protective effect in humans and animals |
| Different drugs (cyclophosphamide, benzoteph, ethimidin, sarcolysin, etc.) | Protective effect in animals |
| Industrial poisons and domestic chemistry (aniline, chlorofos, etc.) | Protective effect in animals |
| Endogenous chemical substances (stress reaction products) | Protection of man, rats, mice and animals under stress at the organism level; normalizing action on nucleic acid synthesis inhibited under stress |

and chronic pregnancy infections, delivery time and postnatal periods in humans. Best of all, it exerted a regulatory action on the fetal growth and development and reduced pregnancy complications overall.

Because Siberian ginseng is capable of increasing the resistance of isolated tissues under thermal and certain chemical exposures, it may play an essential role in our new methods of fertilization of humans. It may even solve organ transplantation problems. The possibilities are limitless, and should be explored as a strategic reserve for health.

Tests with farm animals produce startling results. Cows give more milk, chicks become fully grown hens in less time than average, bees increase their production of honey by 30 to 60 percent, incubative quality of eggs improve; percentage of hatched chicks is higher. Resistance of fowl against low temperatures is bolstered. Sexual strength in bulls increases, making them more serviceable for artificial insemination in controlled breeding. Productivity and health invariably improve when Siberian ginseng is administered to rabbits, swine, horses, deer, and dogs.[46-48]

Siberian ginseng may play a powerful role in helping us to withstand increasing exposures to radiation. Radiation is more than fallout from nuclear accidents: It is X-rays, microwaves, television, radar waves, the video display before me—an endless list of high-technology devices. Soviet researcher A. V. Topchiev claims that everyone in the world already has dangerous amounts of radioactive strontium 90 in their bones.

The antioxidant action of Siberian ginseng may be the reason that it extends life. Nine-month-old rats were divided into two groups; one group used as a control, the other receiving Siberian ginseng in drinking water. This procedure continued for almost a year. When half the rats died, the average lifespan of the control group was 680 days, and 800 days for the treated group. When all the test animals were no longer alive, the difference in their lifespan was shown to have increased by 10 percent.

Perhaps we will begin to see application of Siberian ginseng in the treatment of over-tired healthy people and those weakened by disease. The research that demonstrates its effectiveness for functional disorders of the nervous system, impotency, mild forms of diabetes, disorders of the cardiovascular system, and general malnutrition are provocative.[49] It should become one of the most comprehensively studied medicinal plants. An ancient form of protection appropriated from the past may help us in the future.

## CONCLUSION

In one of my good-health fantasies, I envision our government encouraging the use of Siberian ginseng to fight flu epidemics, instead of pushing deadly flu shots. Accumulated data reflect the anti-influenza action of Siberian ginseng. How much wiser to use a natural plant product!

Over a billion dollars a year is currently spent on over-the-counter drugs to alleviate symptoms caused by respiratory ailments alone. (In Russia, 73 percent of similar prescriptions are herbal remedies.)

We now know that cancer and diet are interrelated. An anti-cancer diet is available. Can you implement such a diet? What is your commitment to changing your lifestyle?

Siberian ginseng—*eleutherococcus senticosus*—is a first-class adaptogen. It builds zest, energy, and endurance; increases mental and physical work ability; helps combat everyday weariness; improves mental and physical reflex action, circulation, resistance to disease, visual and hearing acuity.

It delivers a therapeutic effect in chronic irritability, depression, and menopausal discomfort. Most of all, it has a remarkable normalizing and protective effect against most types of stress, and an incremental effect is gained from long-term use. The Japanese sometimes refer to ginseng as *mind-sin*, "best of plants", or *nind-sin*, "wonder of the Universe". It can help to create harmony with your environment, despite powerful man-made chemical and physical challenges.

Many aspects of modern therapies have been disappointing. "Establishment" stimulants and pain relievers come with a price to pay. The drugs of modern medicine—if they work—have side effects. *Eleutherococcus senticosus* has traveled to the moon and to the ocean bottom. It is consumed by yuppies in midtown Manhattan and by peasants in remote provinces of China. Reports of its rewards have been objective and measurable. Let's learn from the past as we bring forth the new—wellness from the wild: earth-plant, Siberian ginseng.

# REFERENCES

1. *Eleutherococcus and Other Adaptogens from Far Eastern Medicinal Plants (Materials Concerning the Studies of Ginseng and Other Medicinal Plants of the Far East,* Issue 7). The Far Eastern Center of the Siberian Division of the USSR Academy of Sciences, Vladivostok, 1966.

2. Brekhman, I. I. *Eleutherococc.* Nauka Publishing House, Leningrad, 1968.
3. Dardymov, I. V., *Ginseng, Eleutherococcus.* Nauka Publishers, Moscow, 1976.

4. Brekhman, I. I. and Dardymov, I. V. "The Mechanism of Increasing the Body Resistance by Ginseng and Eleutherococcus." In: *Protein Synthesis and Cell Resistance.* Nauka Publishers, Leningrad, 1971.

5. National Institute for the Control of Drug and Biological Products and Institute of Botany, Academia Sinica. *Manual of Identifying Chinese Materia Medica,* vol. 1. Scientific Publishing House, Beijing, 1972.

6. Morozova, G. I., Barenboim, G. M., and Dobretsov, G. E. "Interaction Between Xenobiotics and Living Cells: Study by the Method of Fluorescent Probes." *Khimikofarmatsevticheskv Journal,* 1982.

7. Suprunov, N. I. and Zorikov, P. S. "The Effect of Eleutherococcus on Egg Production in Laying Hens, on the Incubative Quality of Eggs, and on the Growth and Development of Young Chicks." The Academy of Sciences of the USSR, Siberian Chapter, Mountain-Forest Station of the Komarov's Far Eastern Branch, 1967.
8. Liapustina, T. A. "The Effect of the Aqueo-Alcoholic Extract from the Roots of Eleutherococcus on incubative Quality of Eggs." The Academy of Sciences of the USSR, Siberian Chapter, Mountain-Forest Station of the Komarov's Far Eastern Branch, 1967.

9. Goldberg, E. E., Shubina, T. S., Sternberg, I. B. "Effect of Eleutherococcus Extract on the Immunological Action of Rubomycin." In: *Problems of Radiobiology and Biological Action of Cytostatic Drugs.* Tomsk University Publishers. Tomsk, 1971.

10 Tsyrlina, E. V. "Effect of Chemotherapeutic Drugs Combined with Eleutherococcus Senticosus Extract on the Origin and Spread of SSK Tumor Metastases." *Voprosy Oncology 11, 1965.*

11. Khatiashvill, T. M. "On the Attempted Employment of *Eleutherococcus* in the Complex Therapy of Cancer of Lip or of Mouth Cavity." *Eleutherococcus and Other Adaptogens.*

12. Yaremenko, K. V. "The Main Aspects of the Use of Eleutherococcus Extract in Oncology." In: *New Data on Eleutherococcus and Other Adaptogens.* The Far Eastern Scientific Center, USSR Academy of Sciences. Vladivostok, 1981.

13. Gvamichava, A. R. et al. "The First Results of the Use of Eleutherococcus in the Combined Treatment of Breast Cancer." In: Materials for Study in: *Eleutherococcus and Other Adaptogens.*

14. Ebert, L. Ya., Broude, A. A., Bukharin, O. V. *Drug Prophylaxis of Infectious Diseases.* South Urals Book Publishers, Chelyabinsk, 1968.

15. Kim et al. "Influence of Ginseng on the Stress Mechanism." Korean Ginseng Studies, Il Hwa Co., Ltd., Seoul, 1977.

16. Bombardelli et al. Proceedings of 3rd International Ginseng Symposium, Korea Ginseng Research Institute, Seoul,1980.

17. Brndis, S. A. and Plilovitzkala, V. N. "On the Efficacy of *Eleutherococcus* Treatment of Men Working Under High Temperature Conditions." In: *Eleutherococcus and Other Adaptogens .*

18. Saratlkov, A. S. "Adaptogenic Action of *Eleutherococcus* and Goldenroot Preparations." In: *Adaptation and Biologically Active Substances.* The Far Eastern Scientific Center, USSR Academy of Sciences, Vladivostok, 1976.

19. Berdyshev, V. V. "Normalization of Seamen's Health Status in the Tropics by Eleutherococcus." In: *Adaptation and Adaptogens.* Far Eastern Book Publishers, Vladivostok, 1977.

20. Tikhomirova, N. M. "Vision analyzer in Seamen Given Adaptogens During Long-Term Navigation". In: *Abstracts of the Reports Made at the 2nd All-Union conference on Human Adaptation to Different Geographical, Climatic and Industrial Conditions.* Siberian Branch, USSR Academy of Medical Sciences. Novosibirsk, 1977.

21. Gagarin, I. A. "*Eleutherococcus* Prophylaxis of the Disease incidence in the Arctic." In: *Adaptation and Adaptogens.* The Far Eastern Scientific Center, USSR Academy of

Sciences. Vladivostok, 1977.

22. Dardymov, I. V. and Khasina, E. I. "The Capacity of Glycosides of Ginseng and Eleutherococcus and Insulin to Prevent the Formation of Inhibitor of Glucose Metabolism in the Blood Under Stress." In: *Adaptation and the Adaptogens.*

23. Bezdetko, G. N., Smolina, T. M., Shulyateva, L. D. "Effects of Ginseng and *Eleutherococcus* Extracts on Alloxan Diabetes in Rats." In *Materials of the Scientific Conference on Pharmacology and Medicinal Application of Eleutherococcus Senticosus.* The Military Faculty of Physical Culture and Sports, P. F. Lesgaft Institute of Physical Culture, Leningrad, 1961.

24. Galanova, L. K. "*Eleutherococcus* in the Prophylaxis of Influenza and Recurrent Essential Hypertension." In: *Adaptation and Adantogens.*

25. Brekhman, I. I. and Kirillov, O. I. "Protective Effect of eleutherococcus Under the Strain Reaction (Stress)." In: *Eleutherococcus and Other Adantogens.*

26. Dardymov, I. V., Asina, E.I., Brekhman, I. I. "The Inhibitory Action of Lipoproteins on Hexokinase Under Stress." In: *Abstracts of the Reports Made at the 3rd All-Union Biochemical Congress.* The institute of Organic Synthesis of the Academy of Sciences of the Latvian SSR, Riga, 1974.

27. Brekhman, I. I . "*Eleutherococcus*: A New Stimulant and Tonic." The V. I. Lenin Military Institute of Physical Culture and Sports, Leningrad, 1960.

28. Bezdetko, G. N. et al. "Study of the Pharmacokinetics and Mechanism of Action of *Eleutherococcus* Glycosides: Incorporation of Tritium to Eleutheroside 6, the Kinetics of its Accumulation and Elimination from the Animal Body." *Khimiko-Pharmatsevtichesky Journal,* 1981

29. Dardymov, I. V. "Material Kizuch, Ahenshenya i Drugiskh Lekarstv. *Rast. Damn. Vost.* Sb. 5,245, 1963.

30. Blokhin, B. N. "Effect of Extracts from the Roots and Leaves of *Eleutherococcus* on the Working Capacity of Athletes." In: *Materials of the 3rd Conference of the Central Research Laboratory of the Tomsk Medical Institute.* Tomsk, 1966.

31. Ovodov, Yu Frolova, G. M., and Elyakova, L. A. "Chemical Study of Glycosides from *Eleutherococcus Senticosus* Rupr. et Maxim and Acanthopanax Sessiliflorus." In: Results of Studies of Eleutherococcus in the Soviet Union. V. L. Komarov Far Eastern Division, Siberian Branch of the USSR Academy of Sciences. Vladivostok, 1966.

32. Shamovsky, I. L. et al. "Evaluation of Certain Characteristics of the Electronic

Structure of Eleutherosides 8, B1, D, and E by the CNDO/S Quantum-Chemical Method." *Khimiko-Pharmatsevtichesky Journal*, 1982.

33. Padkin, V. V. and Baburin, E. F. "The Excretion of Vitamins Under the Conditions of Joint and Separate Treatment of Men with Eleuterococcus and Polyvitamin Complex." In: *Eleutherococcus and Other Adaptogens.*

34. Brekhman, I.I. and Dardymov, I. V. "A Stimulating Action of individual Glycosides of *Eleutherococcus*." In: 3rd Conference of the Central Research Laboratory.

35. Kaplan, E. Ya. "Prophylactic Effect of *Eleutherococcus* Under the Cerebral injury in Animals." *Eleutherococcus and Other Adaptogens.*

36. Fulder, S. "The Drug that Builds Russians." *New Scientist*, 1980.

37. Kamen, B. Germanium: A New Approach to Immunity. Nutrition Encounter, Larkspur, CA, 1987.

38. Siegel, R. K. "Ginseng Abuse Syndrome." *Journal of the American Medical Association*, 1979.

39. Dyban, A. P. *Abnormal Development of Animal and Human Embryos.* Znanie Publishers, Moscow, 1976.

40. Bezdetko, G. H. "Pharmacological Regulation of the Biosynthesis of Nucleic Acids Under Stress." In: Adaptation and Adaptogens. The Far Eastern Scientific Center of the USSR Academy of Sciences. Vladivostok, 1977.

41. Asimov, M. M. et al "Effect of *Eleutherococcus Senticosus* Glycosides on Early Embryogenesis of the Urchin." *Izvestia ANSSSR* (biological series), 1973.

42. See Reference 40.

43. Bolkhoitinova, S. S. and Zvereva, L. A. "Application of Eleutherococcus for Antenatal Prophylaxis of Embryonal Hypotrophy." In: New Data on Eleutherococcus.

44. Chebotar, N. A. and Gordeichuk, T. N. "Effect of Eleutherococcus on Embryotoxicity of Different Teratogens." In: *New Data on Eleutherococcus.*

45. Dyban, A. P. "Abnormal Development of Animal and Human Embryos." Znanie Publishers, Moscow, 1976.

46. Darkymov, I. V. and O.I. Kirillov, "The Difference in the Weight of Certain Viscera of Young Rats Under the Effects of *Eleutherococcus* and Testosterone Being Administered in the Doses Increasing at Equal Rate Gain in Weight in the Animals." *Eleutherococcus and Other Adaptogens.*

47. Dardymov, I. V. and O.I. Kirillov, "On the Mechanism of Eleutherococcus's Property to increase Gain in Weight in Animals." *Eleutherococcus and Other Adantogens.*

48. Articles by N. I. Suprynov and P. S. Zorikov, T. A. Liapustina, N. I. Suprunov, G.I. Gorshkov and M. S. Antrushin, published by The Academy of Sciences of the USSR, Siberian Chapter, Mountain-Forest Station of the Komarov's Far Eastern Branch.

49. Articles by Iu. N. Yegorov and E.F. Baburin, T.I. Strokina and T.B. Mukho, T.I. Strokina, A.P. Golkhov, and R.I. Mikunus, V.K. Serkova and T.A. Shirkova in *Eleutherococcus and Other Adaptogens.*